DO DINOSAURS MAKE GOOD PETS?

Dr Dino's Learnatorium

DINO

Published by Dino Books,
an imprint of John Blake Publishing Ltd,
3 Bramber Court, 2 Bramber Road,
London W14 9PB, England

www.johnblakebooks.com

www.facebook.com/johnblakebooks 🅵
twitter.com/jblakebooks 🅴

This edition published in 2015

ISBN: 978 1 78418 652 4

British Library Cataloguing-in-Publication Data:

A catalogue record for this book is available from the British Library.

Design by www.envydesign.co.uk

Printed in Great Britain by CPI Group (UK) Ltd

1 3 5 7 9 10 8 6 4 2

Papers used by John Blake Publishing are natural, recyclable products made
from wood grown in sustainable forests. The manufacturing processes conform
to the environmental regulations of the country of origin.

Every attempt has been made to contact the relevant copyright-holders,
but some were unobtainable. We would be grateful if the
appropriate people could contact us.

Introduction

Welcome, children (and any adults who want to come along as well) to my wonderful learnatorium, a place where myself – the famous T-rex Dr Dino with a PhD in Universal Knowledge – and my Assistant Learnatours attempt to teach people all about the wonders of the universe.

This particular book was an extremely difficult one for me to write. Although I love to teach humans all about the prehistoric world and the greatest animals to ever walk the Earth (dinosaurs, of course!), it is always hard for me to think about what a wonderful place the Earth was sixty-five million years ago, compared to the world ruled by mammals that we live in today.

However, this was an important book to write because there is so much misinformation out there about dinosaurs – and those that lived with them and came afterwards – which has almost certainly been spread by your teachers, and which I have to correct.

Don't get me wrong. Some teachers are excellent and will try to teach you as best as they can, but they normally focus on the truly boring facts when they could be telling you about the enormous shark – over twice as big as any shark alive today – that used to rule the ocean. Or about dinosaurs whose feathers helped them to run vertically up trees. Or even about the tuatara, a type of lizard which has been around for over 200 million years and is still alive today (obviously not the exact same one as was alive 200 million years ago... not even my facts are *that* amazing).

Of course, dinosaurs were around over 200 million years ago, and the Earth itself is *waaaaay* older than that, so it's impossible to teach you about everything and everyone. I could write an entire book solely about my own T-rex species, for example. We're just dipping our toes into the prehistoric world in all its glory, but I hope that you will be so excited by it that you will want to go and do research on it all by yourself. And if you do, then see if you can pop over to my learnatorium. Visitors are always welcome, especially if they like dinosaurs!

Dr Dino

In the Beginning

4.54 billion years. That's how old the Earth is! But it hasn't always looked the way it does now. Think about the oldest, crustiest teacher you have… do you think they have always looked that old and crusty? No, even if it might seem that way, they haven't.

The difference is that, while your teacher has become grey, haggard, and probably with hair growing out of all sorts of places it shouldn't, the Earth is now beautiful, with deep blue seas and luscious green jungles. But when it was first created it wasn't the sort of place you would have liked to be living at all.

The Earth now   Your teacher now   The Earth then

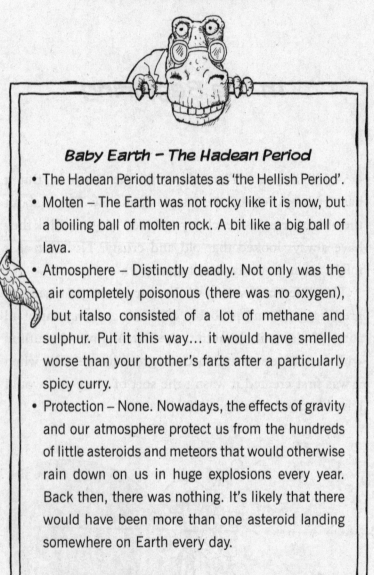

Baby Earth – The Hadean Period

- The Hadean Period translates as 'the Hellish Period'.
- Molten – The Earth was not rocky like it is now, but a boiling ball of molten rock. A bit like a big ball of lava.
- Atmosphere – Distinctly deadly. Not only was the air completely poisonous (there was no oxygen), but italso consisted of a lot of methane and sulphur. Put it this way… it would have smelled worse than your brother's farts after a particularly spicy curry.
- Protection – None. Nowadays, the effects of gravity and our atmosphere protect us from the hundreds of little asteroids and meteors that would otherwise rain down on us in huge explosions every year. Back then, there was nothing. It's likely that there would have been more than one asteroid landing somewhere on Earth every day.

When the Earth first formed, it didn't have a moon. In fact, the Moon formed quite late, about sixty million years after the Earth. Over the years, many people have tried to explain the Moon and how it got there, and there have been some pretty wacky theories put forward by humans ... not least the one where people believe that the Moon is an abandoned spaceship!

The most likely explanation scientists have come up with is pretty cool though. It's called the Giant Impact Hypothesis, and the idea is that another planet the size of Mars smashed into the Earth one day. It's hard to imagine how big the explosion was, but it would have been more

than one billion times bigger than a nuclear bomb – so big that, if it happened now, the entire world would melt!

In the course of the explosion a chunk of the Earth was blown right off, and when the space dust had quite literally settled, *voila!* There was the Moon.

Back in those days, not only was the grass not green (there was no grass – life hadn't formed yet), but also the sky wasn't blue. Because the Earth's atmosphere hadn't formed yet, everywhere would probably have simply been black.

Over time, and by 'time' I mean almost one billion years – which is a long time even by dinosaur standards – the Earth cooled, oceans began to form and clouds would

have started floating around the sky. Earth still wouldn't have been a pleasant place, though, because if you weren't getting rained on by corrosive acid, you would have been either freezing your bottom off or boiling to death – by now the Earth would most likely have been an ice planet with a lot of very active volcanoes. And what's more, the smell wasn't getting any better.

Fortunately, there was nothing alive on Earth to worry about all of those problems. Nothing, that is, until…

Life!

It is one of the great unsolved scientific mysteries: how was life formed? Even in my great learnatorium, my Assistant Learnatours and I are unable to create molecules as complex as those that make up even simple life.

Then again, I don't have hundreds of millions of years to get it right. I'm sure if I did then I could crack it.

Life began with very simple single-celled organisms – meaning that they were so tiny that their whole 'body' was literally just one cell. To put that into context, a human is about 100 trillion cells (and a T-rex is a whole lot more), so these little critters don't seem all that special. But they were!

So far, the Earth is the only place in the universe where we know that life exists. Although most scientists, including myself, the great Dr Dino, think that the universe is most likely teeming with life throughout all of its galaxies, for now the Earth is the liveliest place in

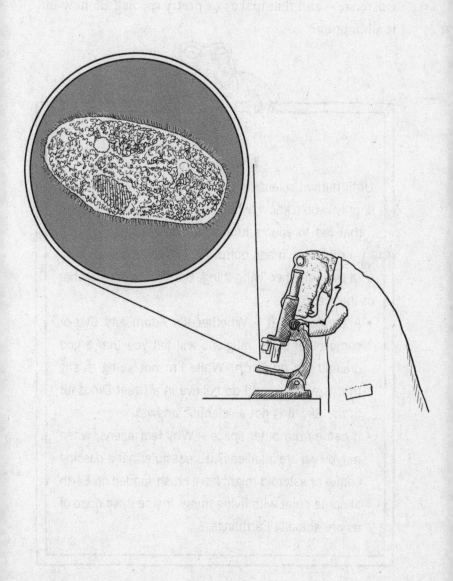

existence – and that makes us pretty special! So how did it all happen?

Living It Up

Until human scientists get their thinking caps on, we simply won't know what started us down the path that led to you, a human, reading a book by me, a dinosaur, made out of paper, which comes from a tree, another living thing. But there are a number of theories:

- A creator did it – Whether it's Adam and Eve or some other story, religions will tell you that a god created life on Earth. While I'm not going to say that is wrong, and I do believe in a Great Dinosaur in the Sky, it is not a scientific answer.

- It came from outer space – Why fear aliens, when maybe we are all aliens? It's possible that a passing comet or asteroid might have crash-landed on Earth at some point with living things inside it, so none of us are actually Earthlings.

- RNA – You will most likely have been told about DNA by your teachers, the complex building blocks that make life. But you may not have heard of RNA, which is like DNA but a bit more simple and easier to make and understand. It's possible that life began only needing the relatively simple RNA, and then *evolved* to have DNA.

- Dumb luck – The chances of life sparking out of nothing are astronomically small, and people argue that it's so unlikely it could never have happened by accident. But people forget that the universe is astronomically big, with more planets than it's possible to imagine. And billions of years is a very, very long time. The most likely explanation is simply that the universe is so vast that an incredibly unusual series of events *has* to happen somewhere, because at some point everything will happen! Imagine this: for life to start, you have to flip a coin one million times, and it has to be heads every time. Never going to happen, right? Wrong... if you can flip the coin infinity times, then at some point it will come up heads one million times in a row. It might sound stupid, but that's science for you!

The oldest living thing, or rather the oldest thing scientists have found that was once alive, is a fossilised 'microbial mat' – a large group of tiny single-celled organisms all living together in a group. It is 3.48 billion years old, only one billion years younger than the Earth itself!

Even though these microbes are only a single cell and don't even have a nucleus (like a cell's brain), they are quite advanced in some ways. We scientists think that life was around for hundreds of millions of years before even this microbial mat.

The Earth has been home to life for almost four billion years, so it's natural to think the world has been teeming with life ever since then. However, life took its time to get going. For three billion years, nothing ever evolved further than only being single cell-sized. It's only

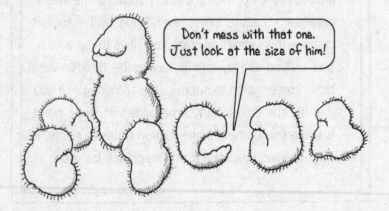

Don't mess with that one. Just look at the size of him!

recently – well, about one billion years ago – that the first organism evolved into something with not one, but two cells. It probably felt as big as I do spending every day surrounded by puny humans.

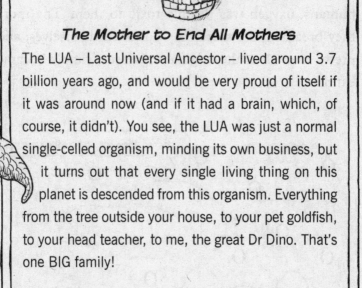

The Mother to End All Mothers

The LUA – Last Universal Ancestor – lived around 3.7 billion years ago, and would be very proud of itself if it was around now (and if it had a brain, which, of course, it didn't). You see, the LUA was just a normal single-celled organism, minding its own business, but it turns out that every single living thing on this planet is descended from this organism. Everything from the tree outside your house, to your pet goldfish, to your head teacher, to me, the great Dr Dino. That's one BIG family!

Oxygen is, of course, key to animals' survival, and we can't live without it for more than a couple of minutes. But the early atmosphere didn't contain oxygen, so how did it get there? Most of the earliest organisms made energy by photosynthesising (meaning that they made energy from carbon dioxide and produced oxygen, which is what plants do now). Gradually, oxygen became a bigger and bigger part of the world – great news for evolution and humans (and the smell)!

Unfortunately, it was very bad news for the organisms already alive... Just as carbon dioxide is poisonous for humans, oxygen was deathly toxic to them. The more they breathed, the more they poisoned themselves, and pretty soon all of the original organisms simply became extinct.

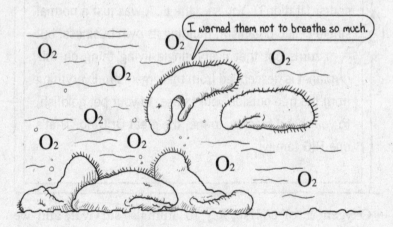

I warned them not to breathe so much.

My Family (and Other Animals)

135,000,000

Forget the Stone Age, the Bronze Age, the Iron Age... The greatest age of all was the Golden Age – the Age of the Dinosaurs. (NOTE: The Golden Age isn't the official scientific name for this period, but I'm lobbying my fellow scientific community hard to change it.) Humans might rule the world right now, but they have only been in charge of the Earth for a few thousand years. Dinosaurs were in charge for 135 MILLION YEARS. So before you humans start to think too much of yourselves, try to remember that you've only been around for a mere blink of the eye compared to the dinos.

My family, the dinosaurs, first appeared around 227 million years ago. I miss those glorious

←200,000

13

days so much! It's a common mistake – one which your teachers are bound to make – to think that all of the dinosaurs appeared at once and all lived together at the same time. That couldn't be more wrong, as you will see if you come to visit my learnatorium. We were around for 160 million years, and that's a very long time, even for a dinosaur, so it's not surprising dinosaurs changed and evolved over that period.

Most of the early dinosaurs were small and quick, like the Chindesaurus, a meat-eating dinosaur about four metres in size with long legs and a whip-like tail. Just like humans, I only know about the Chindesaurus from fossils, because the last one died about 210 million years ago, and the first Tyrannosaurus rex wasn't born until 67 million years ago – so we missed each other by over 140 million years!

Dr Dino's Enormous Eras

Geologists and palaeontologists – scientists who study the ancient Earth and dinosaurs – have to deal with long periods of time. After all, we aren't talking about decades or centuries, or even millennia... we're talking hundreds of millions of years. So they've come up with a handy way of dividing up time into different eras, and if you want to be a dino expert like one of my Assistant learnatours, who help me in my learnatorium, then you'd better remember these!

Triassic – 251 million years ago to 199 million years ago. The Triassic period started right after the Great Dying, which was a terrible period for the Earth: ninety-five per cent of all species of plants and animals became extinct! However, that made room for the rise of the dinosaurs, so it wasn't all bad, although at this time dinosaurs weren't the top dogs (or reptiles) on the planet. Most dinosaurs at this time were relatively small, while the world was very big – all of the land on Earth was joined into one gigantic super-continent called Pangea.

Jurassic – You will certainly have heard of the Jurassic period because of the successful, but very unscientific, *Jurassic* films (more on those later – I hate people being unscientific at the best of times, but when it comes to dinosaurs...). The Jurassic period came after the Triassic one and continued until 145 million years ago, and for those wonderful fifty-five million years, dinosaurs ruled the world. They weren't alone though, because mammals (which eventually led to you humans), birds, reptiles and all sorts of other critters were wandering the Earth alongside us.

Cretaceous – The Cretaceous was the longest period of the dino domination, lasting seventy-nine million years until sixty-six million years ago, but it was also the saddest time of all. My brilliant family, the Tyrannosaurus rex, had been around for just two million years (we developed very late, in dinosaur terms) when disaster struck and a great extinction occurred, wiping the dinosaur race off the face of the Earth. The world has never been as good since.

Knowing these different eras may not seem important now, but if you really want to get to know about dinosaurs then this is crucial knowledge.

Before we delve any deeper into the secrets of the prehistoric zone of my learnatorium, we should go over some dino basics, because your teachers will probably have told you a number of incorrect things about my family, and it's up to me to correct them.

Did Humans Live with Dinosaurs?

NO! And any films, TV shows, books or anything else that tells you different is wrong. About sixty-five million years separate the end of the Age of the Dinosaurs from the first human. Of course, I live quite happily alongside other humans, but that's because I'm a peaceful and wise T-rex. Not all of my ancestors were as calm as I am, so it's probably a good thing for humans that they weren't around when dinosaurs were.

Were Dinosaurs Alone on the Earth?

Far from it. Although dinosaurs were the dominant species, just like humans are now, they shared the Earth with all sorts of creatures. Early mammals, reptiles like crocodiles, insects and all kinds of other creatures lived at that time as well. In fact, dinosaurs are just part of a larger group called archosaurs, and there were many different 'saurs' running around with them – and they have often been mistaken for dinosaurs.

The most famous case of stolen dino identity is the

pterodactyl, which you will probably have been taught by your teacher was a flying dinosaur. Wrong! It's actually a pterosaur, of course. Just don't ask for the difference between a dinosaur and a pterosaur because the answer is complicated and, quite honestly, boring. Even to me, and I'm a dinosaur!

How Big Were Dinosaurs?

Humans think of dinosaurs as being enormous, and some, like me, are very big. However, while there were some absolute giants who could squish a human with one large foot, the majority were much smaller – mostly

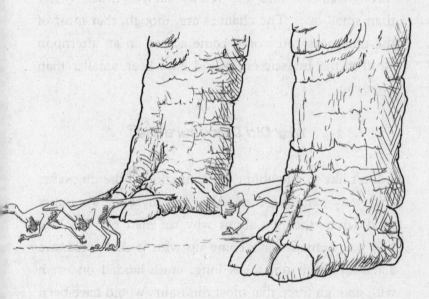

only one metre long, for example. It's hard for humans to know exactly how many dinosaurs were that small, for the simple reason that you learn about dinosaurs through fossils, and big fossils survive much better than small ones. The chances are, though, that most of the dinosaurs you would come across on an afternoon stroll in the Jurassic era would have been smaller than even you.

Why Did Dinosaurs Die?

I don't like to talk about the extinction of the dinosaurs – it's very painful for me. Although there are a number of different theories about why we died off, the best one you humans have come up with is that a massive asteroid, about ten miles long, crash-landed on earth with enough force that most dinosaurs would have been killed immediately in the explosion. Any that managed to survive would have died off later in the decades-long 'winter' that the extra ash and space debris in the atmosphere would have caused.

A truly awful end to a splendid species.

Was That the End of the Dinosaurs?

Well, it can't have been, because I'm here writing this book and teaching humans the wonders of the universe in my learnatorium! But I'm something of a special case, of course.

However, I'm technically not the only dinosaur around on Earth today. In fact, there are far more dinosaurs than there are humans! Every bird you see has evolved from a branch of dinosaurs hundreds of millions of years ago, and they are, scientifically

speaking, still dinosaurs – which makes me feel a lot less lonely. And it means that if you've ever had a pet parrot or budgie then you've actually had a pet dinosaur!

Post-Dinosaur Pandemonium Part One

After the worst period in the Earth's history – the dinosaurs' catastrophic extinction – came a lot of opportunities for all sorts of animals to take their place and try their hands, paws, claws and whatever else they had, at being the top animal on Earth. Here's a selection, which I've split into three chapters, of my favourite animals who came after my family. (This list could go on forever – there have been millions of different and exciting species over the years. If you want to come and do some of your own research, feel free to visit my learnatorium.) Unfortunately, these animals are all now extinct… although after reading a bit about them you might be quite happy about that!

Gastornis – This six-foot tall prehistoric bird certainly wasn't the biggest meat-eating bird, but it might have been one of the most dangerous. Alive about fifty million years ago, it reminds me a bit of myself, with enormously powerful legs and jaws (and teeth!) but small arms. Some scientists have thrown up theories that it might have actually been vegetarian, but I think they are just jealous of how powerful its bite was and how much like a T-rex it was too.

Diprotodon – This marsupial – what we scientists call mammals who carry their babies in pouches, like kangaroos – only died off around 46,000 years ago, probably killed by humans hunting it for its meat! It was basically a giant wombat, and it was the largest marsupial that the Earth has ever seen, growing to about three metres long. Fortunately for the hunting humans, it was a herbivore, so it didn't eat meat, which made their job a lot easier!

Plesiadapis – Living around sixty million years ago, this was one of the earliest primates and therefore an ancestor of you, most likely. A funny-looking creature, it had the head of a rat but the body of a lemur and teeth suited to gnawing on anything from nuts and seeds to insects and small animals.

Glyptodon – This giant armadillo lived in swampy South America and survived for around two million years until just 10,000 years ago. The main difference between the glyptodon and modern-day armadillos was its size... it could grow to ten feet long! Despite being a giant, it was fairly timid and rather than fight it would curl up under its enormous and spiky shell for protection. That obviously wasn't enough, though, because humans hunted the glyptodon to extinction – and to add insult to injury, not only did the humans eat the glyptodons, but they also used the shells as huts to live in!

Anthropornis – Nowadays, penguins are cute fluffy little animals that spend their days sliding on ice and diving for fish. The anthropornis was an entirely different creature: a giant penguin that could grow to two metres tall and weighed as much as 200 pounds, basically the size of a tall human. Luckily for humans, this giant bird also munched on fish, not mammals, and lived about forty-five million years ago.

Embolotherium – These giant mammals lived forty million years ago and looked truly fearsome. A little like rhinos today, they grew three metres high and six metres long, and had a massive bony horn growing on their nose which gave them their name; 'embolotherium' translates to mean 'battering ram beast'. Although you wouldn't have wanted to get in the way of one while it was charging, these beasts were also herbivores, so their bark was worse than their bite. Although the bite was still pretty bad.

Dromornis – The dromornis is closely related to the duck and the goose, but if you came across it at the duck pond you would undoubtedly turn tail and run the other way! It was around for fifteen million years and only died off about 30,000 years ago, and it only really lived in Australia, but it grew to three metres tall and while it didn't have powerful claws like I do (which makes typing very difficult, let me tell you) its beak was so strong it could crush a human skull in an instant.

Pristichampsus – Although the most important reptiles – dinosaurs – all died off in the great extinction event of sixty-five million years ago, there was one type of reptile that thrived, and indeed is still thriving today: the crocodile. The pristichampsus was a type of crocodile that carried on the good work of the dinosaurs, namely eating mammals. This ten-foot-long croc was different from those found today because it was adapted to live on land, with hooves for example, and lived in the jungle where it scuttled around looking for prey. While normally walking on all fours, when sprinting it would rear up onto two legs, which would make it a three-metre-tall eating machine – pretty terrifying to think about (for mammals at least)!

Phiomia – This animal was the first to start growing a trunk, and it was the beginning of a line of creatures that led to the modern-day elephant. Growing to about three metres tall, it only had a small trunk and short tusks – an elephant would probably be embarrassed to be seen with a trunk that small nowadays. Nevertheless, these forty million-year-old beasts could still pack quite a punch if they charged at you.

Rhamposuchus – The largest crocs around today can grow to around six metres long, but that's nothing compared to the rhamposuchus. This reptile lived around twenty million years ago and could grow to a whopping twelve metres, twice as big as the biggest crocodiles now. It looked a bit like a giant gharial, an animal which is around today, and just its snout alone would have been over a metre long and filled with sharp teeth. A frightening proposition for anything swimming in rivers and swamps twenty million years ago!

The Earth Moves

It's very easy to think of the Earth as unchanging. After all, if you leave a house, a stadium, a learnatorium or anything else then you know that when you come back it will be right there where you left it. And the same goes for hills, mountains, lakes and rivers. Unfortunately, all of that is wrong. The Earth is actually moving the whole time – and I'm not just talking about the 67,000 miles per hour that we are flying through space at.

Underneath your feet, and my claws, is a huge boiling, bubbling mass of magma, which is rock and metal that is constantly shifting around. I won't get into too many of the boring details – I'll leave that to your teachers – but the Earth is a little bit like an onion, with many layers: the crust, the mantle, the outer core and the inner core.

Crust
Upper Mantle
Lower Mantle
Outer core
Inner core

Core, Blimey!

Because of clever scientists like me, we know quite a lot about the centre of the Earth – what we scientists call the core – even though it is impossible to drill into it. If you did try to dig to the other side of the world then you had better be ready for some pretty warm temperatures... The centre of the Earth is 6,000 degrees Celsius! That's hotter than the surface of the sun!

Incredibly, research in my Learnatorium and elsewhere shows that the inner core is most likely solid iron. While iron would normally easily melt at such high temperatures, it doesn't in the core – partly because the pressure there is 3.5 million times greater than it is on the Earth's surface.

So if you did manage to dig the whole way there it would be a close race between what would happen first. Would you get burned to a crisp, or crushed like you were an empty crisp packet? Unless you want to volunteer to be the guinea pig for the experiment, then I don't think we will ever know.

Because of the way that the Earth is built, the mantle creates convection currents (very hot and powerful blasts of air) which are so strong that they actually cause the crust of the Earth to move. Of course, it doesn't move very quickly – you would notice it if it did – but on average the surface of the Earth shifts about an inch every year.

And it doesn't all move the same way. The Earth's surface is made up of different 'plates' and each of these plates move in different directions.

But why, you ask, am I, the great Dr Dino, talking about the way the Earth is built in a book about prehistoric history? Well, the Earth's geology (which is the scientific name for the study of the way it is formed) is one of the most important factors in life and evolution. Without it, life simply couldn't survive.

When the Earth cooled billions of years ago, the surface formed a rocky crust and broke up into the moving plates. As these plates move they bump into each other and pull apart, which causes all sorts of things to happen, including bumps and dips on the surface... or as you humans like to call them: mountains and oceans. And where did life form? In the oceans! Without those vast pools of water, it's unlikely that life could ever have formed.

Geology has a downside too. When two enormous

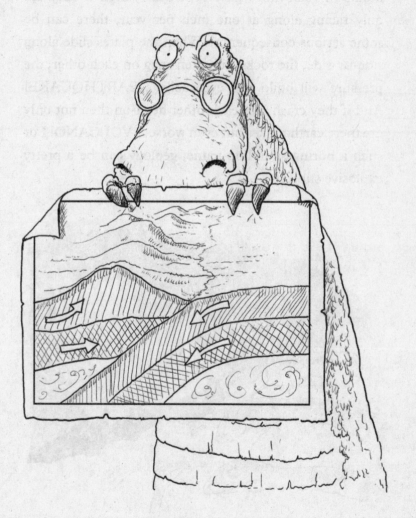

hunks of rock move past each other, even if they are only racing along at one inch per year, there can be some serious consequences. When the plates slide along side-by-side, the rocks will often snag on each other, the pressure will build and eventually... EARTHQUAKE! And if they crash into each other head-on then not only are there earthquakes but even worse... VOLCANO! For such a boring sounding name, geology can be a pretty explosive subject.

While humans might think volcanoes to be just a little bit of a nuisance, over the years they haven't been very helpful to life on Earth. In fact, more than once in the Earth's history, life has almost been wiped out by the eruption of super-volcanoes, which spewed out so much ash when they erupted that the entire world has been plunged into a winter that lasts decades.

Terrifying Toba

Whenever I feel my brain overheating, which is quite often because of how large it is, I take the opportunity to go to one of my favourite places on Earth: a beautiful lake in Indonesia 100 kilometres long and thirty kilometres wide called Lake Toba. But while it's beautiful now, I wouldn't have liked to have been there 70,000 years ago.

The entire lake was the crater of a huge super volcano, and when Toba erupted 70,000 years ago it caused a severe winter around the world for a decade. Not only that but, for the next 1,000 years, the Earth was cooler than it should have been. Unlike when other major eruptions occurred, 70,000 years ago humans were around, and life is tough for a caveman when it's a bit chilly outside!

In fact, life was so tough that humans very nearly became extinct. From studying genetic DNA, scientists like me have figured out that the human population dropped to around 3,000 people after the Toba eruption, which is about as close to extinction as it's possible to get!

The Earth's constant shifting might seem like a nuisance, but there's one other extremely important job it does – and unless you've previously visited my learnatorium, you almost certainly won't guess what it is: electro-magnetism.

The inner core of the Earth is solid, but the outer core is liquid and constantly spinning. This movement creates an electromagnetic field around the Earth – which might not seem important, but it is. Space is a scary place, and one of the most dangerous things in it is solar radiation, and if humans are exposed to that for any length of time it means certain death. The electromagnetic field is like a force field around the Earth protecting it, and all life on it, from this radiation. Without it, life as we know it could never have been created.

If you were to look at any of my dinosaur maps that I keep in my Learnatorium you would be incredibly confused, and not just because they are written in Dinosaurus, the official language of the dinosaur world. As the plates move, so does all the land on them, which is why, when dinosaurs first evolved, all of the land on Earth was joined up in one big super-continent. Over a very long time, all of the continents have drifted around until they are in the shape you see today, but they are still drifting even now.

As you read this, Africa is slowly marching towards Europe, and vice versa, and in fifty million years or so they should smash together. At the same time, the Americas and Europe are drifting further and further apart.

In about 250 million years or so, all of the continents will finally join forces once more and come together to form another super-continent. I can only hope that when that happens it will lead to the rise of the dinosaur race again, just like it did last time...

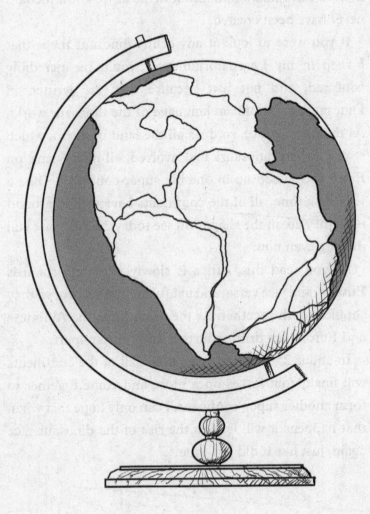

The Dinocyclopedia
Part One

Dinosaurs, as we have seen, were around for 160 million years, and a lot of changes happened over that time. Many species of dinosaur came and went naturally, long before the great extinction of sixty-five million years ago. The sheer variety of dinosaurs was simply wonderful – thinking about all of my fellow dinos makes me extremely happy, and just a little bit hungry... I can't help it, it's a natural reaction. I am a T-rex after all! There are far too many dinosaurs, literally thousands of them, to go into here – just like the post-dinosaur animals. If you want to learn more then come on over to my learnatorium – but some of the best can be found here:

Allosaurus (name means 'Different Lizard') – Living in the late Jurassic period, around 150 million years ago, the Allosaurus is one of the best-known dinosaurs, partly because there have been so many of its fossils found, and partly because it is simply one of the best carnivorous dinosaurs around. Growing to five metres tall and thirteen metres long, it probably weighed 1,500 kilograms and really threw its weight about! The number of injuries found on the fossils show that it got itself into a lot of fights, using its strong arms, dozens of sharp teeth and horned head to great effect. And it didn't bother with fighting any of the smaller dinos either – its arch-nemesis was the Stegosaurus, and when those two got into a fight it was really a sight, much more exciting than any of the so-called heavyweight fights you humans take part in.

Deinonychus ('Terrible Claw') – Living between 120 and 110 million years ago, the Deinonychus only grew

to around three metres and mainly ate plants, but also small plant-eating dinosaurs. It was these dinos that the Velociraptors of *Jurassic Park* were based on. Swift, vicious and agile, they darted around and changed direction by flicking their rigid tails behind them. Although their front claws were fairly useless (and their arms may have actually been permanently crossed) their legs were incredibly strong, and their claws were sharp and powerful – they often pinned their prey with these 'terrible claws' and gobbled them down before the captured animal knew what was happening.

Parasaurolophus ('like "Saurolophus"') – A good-sized dinosaur at ten metres in length and 3,500 kilograms in weight, the Parasaurolophus was a herbivore that lived about seventy-five million years ago. It had a big body with a very heavy tail, which it would swing around violently to protect itself when attacked, and a bill similar to a duck's (although it was in no way a giant duck!), but most bizarrely it also sported a huge narrow crest at least a couple of metres long that grew from the back of its head. Initially, stupid human palaeontologists believed that it was an aquatic dinosaur and the crest was used as

a snorkel, but they were way off. If they had asked me I could have told them that the Parasaurolophus lived on land in herds and actually used the crest to shout across to their mates. They were unbelievably noisy, believe me!

Troodon ('Wounding Tooth') – Descended from crocodilians themselves, these dinosaurs eventually became modern-day birds! Troodons laid eggs in their nests just like birds do nowadays, sitting on them to keep them warm. It walked on two legs, was about two metres long, was probably feathered and had sharp, curved teeth which gave it its name. It also had advanced eyes, with binocular vision that may also have made it able to see in the dark, and it had one more very important feature – an enormous brain! You mammals love to brag about how big your brains are, but the Troodon was quite possibly the smartest dino around (until me, of course...) and could have given mammals a run for their money.

Utahraptor ('Utah's Predator') – This raptor was probably the biggest raptor to have lived, at about eighteen feet from tail to tip, living about 125 million years ago, long before the Velociraptor, for example. It was covered in feathers, and it used these to help it run right up the sides of trees! Although we can't be sure

whether it hunted in packs or by itself, we do know that it had incredibly fierce claws on its feet and could probably smell its prey from about a mile away! Imagine how far away it could smell your dad's socks...

Dilophosaurus ('Two-ridged Lizard') – A quick, carnivorous dinosaur living about 190 million years ago, the Dilophosaurus was about twenty feet long, weighed 400 kilograms and had plenty of very sharp, curved teeth. It had bony ridges in its head (hence the name) and a weird kink in its jaw, which was quite a lot like a crocodile's and makes scientists think that it was possibly a fish-eater, rather than a hunter on land. The important thing to know about this dinosaur, however, is not to listen to Steven Spielberg about it! *Jurassic Park* showed the Dilophosaurus as about the size of a dog, able to spit poison and with a frightening neck frill that it fanned out when scared. In reality, it had none of those things, and was about ten times the size!

Apatosaurus ('Deceptive Lizard') – You may well have heard of the Brontosaurus, which is more famous than the Apatosaurus, but unfortunately it never existed. Some silly human scientist misidentified an Apatosaurus, and thought he'd found an entirely new species! He hadn't... very deceptive indeed! It lived between 147 and 137 million years ago and was absolutely gargantuan, even compared to me. It grew up to twenty-one metres long, with a very long neck and a long whippy tail, and weighed up to forty tons. As well as getting this herbivore's name wrong, some scientists believed that it lived underwater, simply because it was so big that they thought it couldn't stand up because it was so heavy. However, as a dinosaur and a doctor, I can tell you they are wrong, and that it lived on land.

Stegosaurus ('Covered Lizard') – This famous dinosaur walked on four legs and could grow up to twelve metres long. The most interesting thing about this giant herbivore, however, was the four rows of armoured plates that ran down its back and through its tail – which was a formidable weapon that had one-metre-long spikes on the end of it and proved mighty effective in its many fights against the Allosaurus. There have been malicious rumours over the years, spread by mammals no doubt, that the Stegosaurus's brain was no bigger than a walnut. That's simply untrue – it was twice the size of a walnut. Which I'll admit isn't all that much better... but it's still something!

More than Monkeys?

In my experience, humans (or should I say *Homo sapiens*, which is the technical scientific name for the human species) like to think of themselves as pretty special. But you humans aren't even reptiles, which is undoubtedly the best type of animal. Instead you are inferior mammals – or at least inferior in my unbiased dinosaur opinion.

Your biology teacher might well teach you the boring facts about mammals: that they are animals that generally have hair or fur, are born alive, are warm-blooded, are fed milk by their mothers and have more complex brains than other animals. (I am currently disputing this last 'fact' with my fellow leading scientists – they only need to come to my learnatorium to examine my brain to realise how wrong they are.)

However, there are 4,200 species of mammals on Earth right now, and hundreds of thousands of species that have already become extinct. They range from the huge – the blue whale, which weighs 190,000 kilograms – to the tiny, like the bumblebee bat which only weighs around two grams. Some have huge tongues, such as the giraffe, whose tongue is so long it can lick the top of its head, and some are a bit excitable, like the Etruscan shrew, whose heart beats twenty-five times every second!

And these mammals all came from somewhere…

Memoirs of a Mammal

Mammals first appeared in the Triassic period, about the same time as early dinosaurs, so they lived side by side with dinosaurs (mainly as their snacks) and have been around for hundreds of millions of years. Over the time that we dinosaurs ruled the Earth, mammals were just puny little rodents, hardly big enough for us to bother eating them in my opinion.

However, when the unthinkable happened and the dinosaurs died out, mammals somehow survived.

Not all of them, but enough that, without any dinosaurs to munch on them, they started to thrive and began the journey towards dominating the world. It was about 400,000 years later that a remarkable little creature came along – the mother of all mammals.

This special animal was the ancestor of all the mammals on Earth today (or at least the ones who don't lay eggs), meaning everything from elephants to cats, humans to bears.

So what was it? A fierce tiger-like creature? A cunning monkey? No, it was a tiny little animal that ate insects and looked like a cross between a rat and a shrew.

So if your teacher tells you that humans are descended from monkeys, tell them they are wrong... you're really descended from rat-like critters who were here sixty-five million years ago!

Although normally it was dinosaurs eating mammals for dinner – the normal order of things – there is evidence that when the two species lived together that wasn't always the case.

The repenomamus lived around 130 million years ago and it was a giant mammal compared to the others around at the time. Shaped a bit like a badger, it could grow up to three feet long and a fossil has been found with chewed-up dinosaur bones inside its stomach... so at least one mammal gave us dinosaurs a bit of a fight then, even if the rest of you were too scrawny to be more than just a mid-afternoon snack.

It always amazes me when humans come visit my learnatorium and they are so proud of being mammals, but they can't even name a single one of their earliest ancestors who lived alongside my family. If you want to impress your friends, teachers, and most importantly, the great Dr Dino, then you should learn about these:

Fruitafossor – The fruitafossor was about six inches long and lived around 150 million years ago. It looked a little like a mole does nowadays and was remarkable for being the first mammal that evolved in order to dig. It may well have lived underground and used its claws to burrow away from approaching hungry dinosaurs. It's just like a mammal to run rather than fight!

Cronopio – This was a small mammal, only a few inches long, but it had a long nose and sharp teeth and has become well-known as the 'sabre-toothed squirrel' of the Cretaceous era. It is a little like Scrat from the incredibly unscientific movie *Ice Age* – unscientific because a sabre-toothed tiger wouldn't be friends with a sloth; he would eat it. Rather than a sweet little creature eating nuts though, a cronopio would actually have been a vicious animal that preyed on insects and other small animals.

Cimolestes – This mammal was a relatively late animal, living about fifty-six million years ago, and it was quite big compared to the other mammals around at the time. In fact, it was so much bigger (still only one kilogram) that it used to run around the treetops eating any other small mammals it found! What's more, cimolestes evolved and it is the ancestor of almost every carnivorous mammal around today, from bears and lions to kittens and puppies.

Agilodocodon – This agile mammal from the Jurassic era 165 million years ago was absolutely tiny, but was probably the first to evolve to climb trees. This was a very important evolutionary step for mammals because, with so many ravenous dinosaurs wandering the Earth's surface, they needed a method of escape so as not to get eaten.

Purgatorius – This was a quite unremarkable six-inch-long mouse-like mammal, with just one exciting feature. Its teeth looked more like a monkey's and it's quite possible that purgatorius is the animal that all humans are descended from, living sixty-five million years ago.

Cimexomys – This rat-like mammal is one of the most despicable of all mammals, and that's saying something! It was about one foot long and it is believed that it used to feed on the poor defenceless eggs of dinosaurs. Horrific, I know!

Oh ... hello, I've just hatched! ... Mummy!

Juramaia – Although it's hard to know for certain, this absolutely miniscule critter may well have been the link between early mammals that gave birth with eggs and mammals that gave birth to live young – the ancestor of all today's mammals that I told you about earlier. It lived 160 million years ago.

Hadrocodium – The hadrocodium was small even for mammals. It was only about an inch long and looked pretty pathetic to be honest. What was surprising about it was how enormous its brain was. Well… it's only one inch in size, so its brain is still tiny, but compared to the rest of its body it is very big, and this quirk was an early indication that you mammals might actually be quite clever one day.

Obviously, these mammals are all pretty similar because while we dinos were around, there wasn't much space for mammals to grow too much. Once tragedy struck and the great race of dinosaurs had died there was a lot more space for mammals, and other types of animals, to grow and evolve. And evolve they did…

The Dinocyclopedia
Part Two

Human palaeontologists have been wrong about dinosaurs an awful lot – considering you regard yourselves as being the smartest animals to have ever lived it's actually quite embarrassing how often you have been wrong. However, at least the scientists are trying to get things right, and I'll admit that analysing fossils is a tricky business – especially when you have claws for hands. It's humans like the Hollywood directors who intentionally get things scientifically wrong that really annoy me, although I do appreciate how much they seem to love us T-rex.

That's why I've started this Dinocyclopedia, so that I can use my PhD in universal knowledge to try to teach people about what dinosaurs were really like. Unfortunately, this book only has a little space, but there is so much more to learn in other books, online or in my learnatorium.

DO DINOSAURS MAKE GOOD PETS?

Archaeopteryx ('First Bird') – Living around 145 million years ago, this particular dinosaur has caused thick-headed humans all sorts of problems. Only about twenty inches tall, with feathered wings which were capable of flight (although it was much better at gliding from tree to tree than actually flapping), when the fossil of this dinosaur was first found it was classified as a bird. Once humans finally realised just how old this dinosaur actually was, they thought that it was the very first bird, or at the very least the last dinosaur just before it evolved into a bird – which, as we know, is still a dinosaur. However, they couldn't have been more incorrect! Although it had many bird-like features, it actually almost certainly evolved into raptors (which humans have finally realised had feathers), rather than into birds. Just another example of why humans need me to help clear things up!

Spinosaurus ('Spine Lizard') – I will admit it, the Spinosaurus isn't my favourite dinosaur. It was a big carnivorous dino. Very big. Bigger than me, much as I don't like to say it. It could grow to eighteen metres in length and had massive spines down its back which formed a very distinctive sort of sail. Living around 100 million years ago, at least no T-rex would have ever had to come across one. However, humans made yet another mistake with this dinosaur. They believed that it was a lumbering dinosaur on land, but what they didn't realise was that the Spinosaurus was actually an aquatic dinosaur, with a jaw that looked very much like that of a crocodile – long, powerful and very sharp. It was, in fact, the very first dinosaur that was able to swim... just another way it had one up on me!

Corythosaurus ('Corinthian-helmet Lizard') – This seventy-five million-year-old dinosaur was a herbivore with a bony protective head which the first human palaeontologists thought reminded them of an ancient Greek helmet, which led to its unusual name. A ten-metre-long herbivore, the Corythosaurus had a duck-bill for a nose and a small(ish) crest on the top of its head which it used to blow air through in order to shout to its fellow dinos. Although they weren't particularly strong (compared to other dinosaurs, that is – compared to humans they were like Superman), they were pretty good endurance runners, so if they got a head start on any predators there was a good chance they could get away.

Psittacosaurus ('Parrot Lizard') – Although there are a whole lot of fossils of this particular dinosaur, it has never been particularly famous with humans, possibly because, apart from having a beak shaped a bit like that of a parrot (which it used to crack open nuts and other tough foods), there wasn't all that much exciting about it. However, with further study it's become apparent that the rest of its head looked a bit like a warthog and its body was covered in prickly hedgehog-like bristles. In addition, while it walked on all four limbs, its back legs simply kept growing throughout its life while its front legs stopped getting larger, meaning the older it got the more lopsided and weird it looked.

Iguanodon ('Iguana Tooth') – The Iguanodon was one of the most successful dinosaurs, surviving for thirty million years between 140 million and 110 million years ago. A massive herbivore, it could grow to ten metres long and weighed as much as 5,000 kilograms. This dino has a special place for humans, as it was only the second dinosaur ever to be discovered. Where its thumb should have been (had it been a human) was a wickedly sharp spike, which it used to defend itself against predators large enough to dare attack it.

Ankylosaurus ('Fused Lizard') – One of the stranger looking dinosaurs, the Ankylosaurus was around at the same time as my fellow T-rexes, from sixty-eight million years ago until the terrible dinosaur extinction. Growing to about six metres long, these short dinosaurs looked a little like armadillos do today, and they were heavily protected by a fused series of bones all over their bodies. Along with the overall covering of armour plating, it also had rows of spikes right down its back, and a tail with a large hammer-like growth at the end, which could be swung very powerfully in defence. Although it wasn't overly aggressive, the Ankylosaurus was built like a tank, and it wasn't a dino I would particularly want to mess with, even though I am a T-rex.

Carnotaurus ('Carnivorous Bull') – Standing at about eight metres long, and living around seventy million years ago, this dangerous dinosaur had even smaller and more embarrassing arms than I do. However, it had a frighteningly powerful jaw, two horns on the top of its head for painful ramming attacks, bumpy skin to hurt anything that ran into it and was one of the fastest dinosaurs around. Probably its only weakness was that because it was so quick it couldn't turn properly – so a swift side-step while being charged could possibly get you out of trouble. All the same, it was probably smartest not to get yourself in that position.

No, really, they're great arms, not at all funny.

Protoceratops ('First Horned Face') – Some human palaeontologists have decided that the Protoceratops was so common that they should call it the sheep of the dinosaur world. But if that's the case then these were pretty tough sheep. Living about eighty-five million years ago, they grew to about two metres long and weighed 400 kilograms. Although they were herbivores they had a big horny beak for a nose – this was pretty sharp and could cause some real damage to any would-be predator looking for some easy sheep-like prey. And they could certainly fight: a fossil has been found of a Protoceratops and a Velociraptor mid-battle. Scientists believe they were duelling to the death when they were covered by a landslide and so their last fight was frozen for all time.

Giganotosaurus ('Giant Southern Lizard') – Living between 100 and ninety-seven million years ago, the Giganotosaurus was one of us T-rex's major rivals. We never met, because they died out thirty million years before the T-rex arrived, but they were our rivals for the biggest dino carnivore. Unfortunately, they win, outweighing us by about 1,000 kilograms and being slightly taller at thirteen metres in length. The Giganotosaurus was even a faster runner, able to run twice as quickly as I can. However, it loses to us where it really counts: in brain power. Its brain is only half the size of ours (about the same size as a banana), so it was a bit of a dumb dino.

Velociraptor ('Swift Robber') – Thanks to Hollywood, there has been an awful lot of false information put out there about Velociraptors. For one thing they were small, about four feet in size. They were hunters, but of small animals, not big ones, because they probably hunted

alone, not in packs. Although they had relatively big brains, they weren't all that intelligent; they certainly didn't have a patch on me. They had colourful feathers, not scaly skin. In fact, they looked more like chickens than reptiles. And they weren't even that speedy... well, compared to humans they were, they could run at about twenty-five miles per hour, but that's slow compared to other dinosaurs. So *Jurassic Park* and Steven Spielberg have a lot to answer for!

Deadlier Than a Dinosaur?

Although the magnificent creatures that were the dinosaurs were the dominant animals for hundreds of millions of years, they weren't by any means alone on the Earth at that time. We have already seen that mammals were beginning to evolve, but what else lived alongside the 'Terrible Lizards' (as we are affectionately known)?

In the Triassic Period, about 245 million years ago, the rise of the archosaur began. Archosaur translates as 'Ruler Lizard' and you might think, 'Hang on, I've never heard of an archosaur before. My teacher has never told me about them – they can't be important, let alone rule over the world, can they?'

The answer is yes, they are very important. I am an archosaur. All dinosaurs are, in much the same way as all humans are mammals. Other archosaurs include pterosaurs, crocodilians, even modern-day birds. It just so happens that dinosaurs were the most famous of the bunch (and rightly so, in my opinion). Especially towards the start of the dinosaurs' existence, there were any number of other archosaurs roaming the Earth, each looking to become the next dominant species.

For example, there were hundreds of different pterosaurs – flying animals whose name means 'Winged Lizard' – who lived very happily alongside dinosaurs and thrived throughout the entire time we were in charge. In fact, I bet you thought that a couple of members of this selection below were actually dinosaurs themselves.

Pterodactylus ('Winged Finger') – There's no such thing as a Pterodactyl! As a scientist I must insist you use its proper name, the Pterodactylus. This was the first of the pterosaur family to be identified, and it's just a little creature, with a wingspan of a little over one metre. When it was first unearthed, the scientists thought it was just a big bat! However, living 150 million years ago, it was actually among the earliest flying carnivorous animals to walk – and fly – the Earth.

Pteranodon ('Winged Toothless') – Quite misleadingly, given how close their names are, the Pteranodon wasn't that closely related to the Pterodactylus (blame the silly human scientists who named them!). Living about

DO DINOSAURS MAKE GOOD PETS?

Bloomin' pterosaurs!

eighty-five million years ago, the male Pteranodon had an enormous wingspan of over six metres, while the female was only around half the size. While neither the Pteranodon nor the Pterodactylus had feathers, the Pteranodon had something the other pterosaur didn't: a large crest rising from the back of the skull. Unfortunately, nobody quite knows what this was for, but it might have been used as a rudder in order to quickly change direction to fly after some prey on the ground. As its name suggests, the Pteranodon was in fact toothless, so it must have gulped down any animals it was eating in one.

Quetzalcoatlus ('Feathered Serpent God') – This beast was the largest pterosaur that ever lived, with a mammoth eleven-metre wingspan, the size of a decent-sized plane. Although it was a reptile, it was actually shaped remarkably like a flying giraffe, with a very long stiff neck protruding from a sizeable body. The unfortunate pterosaur became extinct with the dinosaurs sixty-five million years ago, but that was probably good news for all of the mammals evolving around that time, as a giant carnivorous reptilian flying giraffe isn't the sort of animal I would want to have to deal with.

Crocodilians were another type of archosaur, and these were very similar in many ways to the crocodilians around today (crocodiles and alligators mainly), which are direct descendants of this ancient bunch. While most haven't changed too much, you will be relieved to know that the Sarcosuchus ('Flesh Crocodile') has. Living 110 million years ago, it grew to twelve metres in length and had an enormous two-metre-long jaw, which was a real crusher. Not only did it have the most devastating bite of any croc ever, it may well be the most powerful one of all time anywhere in the world! Although it mainly chomped on fish to fuel its gigantic body, there was also a suggestion that it would pick fights with the strongest

dinos out there, like the Spinosaurus, in a winner-takes-all (of the meat) battle.

Dr Dino's Super Survivors

Although crocodilians survived the dino extinction of sixty-five million years ago, they have changed a bit (although not a lot) since then. There is one that has remained exactly the same for 200 million years, though: the tuatara, a two-foot-long lizard-like reptile which lives on several small islands off the coast of New Zealand.

While there aren't many other animals around that are exactly the same as they were sixty-five million years ago, there are plenty that are very similar, such as bees, crabs, clams, cockroaches, snails, anteaters, the duck-billed platypus, lobsters, turtles and even some sharks. So perhaps the world we live in now isn't really all that different from the one sixty-five million years ago.

Then again, after reading about some of the other animals in this book, maybe it is!

As well as the large archosaurs that wandered the Earth side-by-side with dinosaurs, there were likely thousands of species of small animals living with them as well. Once more, it would be impossible to name them all, but one example is the cynodonts, a group of tiny reptiles that had very mammal-like features (they looked like rats) – and in fact it was from this group of cynodonts that mammals eventually evolved. Sphenodonts were the better sort of reptiles, lizard-like rather than mammal-like, and although these lovely little critters have almost all died out (the tuatara of New Zealand is the last survivor) there were all sorts running around under the feet of the bigger dinosaurs.

And then, of course, just like today there were insects buzzing around everywhere, although they were rather bigger and decidedly more vicious than the ones humans have to deal with nowadays.

All in all, the Dinosaur Age was a wonderful time of diversity and happiness for all… as long as you were top of the food chain, which luckily T-rex are!

Post-Dinosaur Pandemonium Part Two

You have already read about giant wombats and crocodiles, early elephants and massive penguins, but there was a lot more besides just those, living in the years between the death of the dinos and the world we know now. Here's a selection of a few more bizarre creatures your teachers probably won't ever have told you about:

Megatherium – Sloths today are cute little creatures who spend most of their time sleeping in trees, and probably the best-known sloth is the one that appears as one of the goofy main characters in *Ice Age*. The megatherium, whose name translates as Great Beast, is a little bit different to that, though. Living for two million years, and only dying out in South America about 8,000 years ago, this gigantic sloth could grow to be six metres long and four metres tall, absolutely dwarfing humans – although still pretty small compared to me. The problem was that because

it was so big, it was extremely slow and it may well be the slowest mammal to have ever lived. Luckily, it was another vegetarian, so it didn't have to chase its prey for dinner, but its speed almost certainly led to its downfall, as it was hunted to extinction by humans.

Pyrotherium – In Greek, 'pyrotherium' means 'Fiery Beast', but unfortunately this isn't because it was an incredible animal that could breathe fire. The real reason is quite boring – the first fossils found were in volcanic rock. In fact this was a relatively unexciting elephant-like herbivore that lived in South America and grew to be about three metres long.

Huge Herbivores

You may have noticed that many of the creatures we've come across so far, especially the biggest ones like the megatherium, are herbivores and didn't eat meat. I personally am disgusted by this... I can't imagine life without great big hunks of meat (cows are the best. I try not to eat humans – they are too bony). You might wonder why there were so many herbivores that developed after dinosaurs became extinct (you might also have noticed that the reptilian crocodiles were good carnivores – it's the mammals who became boring herbivores). There's a simple answer for this: grass.

Although there was a little grass around sixty-five million years ago when my family was still alive, it was quite rare, and it was only about ten million years later that grass became abundant and swept around the world. With so much more vegetation to eat, massive herbivores could evolve.

It's just a shame that didn't happen while my family was around, because a six-metre megatherium would have made a fantastic feast for us.

Phosphatherium – This prehistoric elephant lived about sixty million years ago, so it was one of the earliest mammals to evolve after the great extinction of the dinosaurs. But if you happened across it nowadays you wouldn't think of it as an elephant... it was only about three feet long and weighed between two and three

kilograms. Despite its miniscule size, this herbivore was the mother of all of the enormous elephants that have roamed the Earth over the years.

Megalania – This may well have been the largest lizard ever to have lived, and it only died out in Australia about 30,000 years ago, so it's quite possible humans came across them at some point. These enormous meat-eaters could grow to about six metres in length and would lie in wait for their prey before ambushing it. And once the megalania had you there was no escape; it had powerfully sharp claws and brutally jagged teeth that would rip you to shreds in an instant. And even worse, it was poisonous, so even if you escaped from its bite for a moment you would still be doomed. Just my kind of animal!

Necrolestes – This small, ugly mole-like animal lived around twenty million years ago, spending most of its time digging in burrows underground and eating any little worms and insects it came across. What was strange about the necrolestes is that for 120 years scientists couldn't figure out what it was – even I was baffled! That is until we realised that they belonged to a group of mammals thought to have become extinct with the dinosaurs forty-five million years previously. So there's

hope for dinosaurs yet! Maybe my fellow dinos are just underground somewhere…

Indricotherium – This was a truly enormous animal. In fact, it was the largest mammal to have ever lived on land, and it looked quite similar to my fellow dinosaurs like the Diplodocus or the Brachiosaurus. It lived between thirty and fifteen million years ago, it could grow to over forty feet long, twenty feet high, and it weighed about 20,000 kilograms! Its skull was relatively small, but still over a metre long. Fortunately for any other animal around at the time, the indricotherium was yet another huge herbivore, so unless you got stepped on there wasn't too much to worry about.

Procoptodon – This animal, a marsupial, is also known as the Giant Short-Faced Kangaroo, which pretty much tells you everything you need to know. The largest kangaroo to have ever lived, it could grow to ten feet tall and packed quite a punch! Not enough, though, to scare the Australian hunters who went after it about 10,000 years ago and hunted it to extinction.

Inkayacu – The inkayacu was an unremarkable penguin in many ways. About twice as big as an Emperor penguin is today, it was sizeable, but not nearly as large as others that existed over the years. What is odd about these Peruvian penguins is that their feathers weren't black-and-white. They were actually red! Scientists, including myself, still haven't quite been able to explain why they would have red feathers, but they certainly would have been a colourful addition to the beach!

Presbyornis – This bizarre creature lived about sixty-five million years ago, right around the time that the dinosaurs passed away. It looked like a cross between a duck (its head and bill), a goose (its body) and a flamingo (its legs). Growing to be about five metres tall, it lived its life in much the same way as ducks do nowadays, waddling around lakes looking for food. Unfortunately for the presbyornis, there were no humans around then to throw bread for them, so they had to make do eating the weeds and vegetation that grew in those days.

The Dinocyclopedia
Part Three

Although humans only discovered what they were less than 200 years ago, dinosaur fossils have been known about for thousands of years. They were almost always referred to as dragon bones in the history books, and were occasionally thought to be the bones of giants, or biblical creatures. It wasn't until the early nineteenth century that William Buckland, a professor at Oxford University and a human I greatly admire, collected enough fossils to make a report in a scientific journal describing a Megalosaurus.

After that, these 'great fossil lizards' became a fashionable area of study, and in 1842 the Englishman Richard Owen came up with the name 'dinosaur', meaning 'terrible lizard'. Soon, fossil hunting became a real craze and the 'bone wars' began: a race between scientists to find newer and better dinosaurs. Of course, as you will learn if you visit my learnatorium, scientific work cannot be rushed because rushing things leads to making mistakes – which, we have already seen, humans made a fair number of when trying to put dinosaur fossils together. And there were far more mistakes than I have mentioned here. In one famous case, a scientist proudly unveiled his newly discovered dinosaur, only to be told that he had put the head where the bum should be!

Nevertheless, overall, humans have done a pretty good job at discovering and classifying a lot of the members of my extended family. And the exciting thing is, with scientific methods constantly improving and more fossils being found almost every day, there's plenty more to discover! Here are a few more entries in my Dinocyclopedia:

Triceratops ('Three-horned Face') – One of the most famous of the dinosaurs, even your teacher should be able to tell you what a Triceratops looked like. With three big horns jutting out from the front of its head and a frill around its neck, this nine-metre-long herbivore lived at the same time as us T-rex did, sixty-seven to sixty-five million years ago. And what's more, we didn't like each other at all, often getting into massive fights – which the T-rex naturally used to win most of the time. The problem is, humans got most of this wrong (except for

the bit about the T-rex not liking the Triceratops...). For a start, it only had two horns, not three – the third horn was really just a long snout. It was also probably not just a herbivore, but more likely an omnivore who ate a bit of everything, including scavenging on other dinosaurs' kills. And even more bizarrely its skin was covered in fist- (or claw-) sized bumps which had little pimples in the middle. All sorts of reasons for these bumps have been put forward, including the theory that a poison was secreted from them. However, the most likely explanation is that the Triceratops was actually covered in spiky hedgehog-like bristles, which would just add to its weird and intimidating appearance.

Oviraptor ('Egg Thief') – This little feathered raptor is the most unfairly named of all of the dinosaurs (at least by humans. We dinos never used such names for each other). When the first Oviraptor was found, it was discovered positioned on top of a group of Protoceratops' eggs, and so it was assumed it had stolen them for food. However, as more and more of these fossils emerged, it became clear that these were actually its own eggs and that it was a great parent that had died trying to protect them... talk about getting the wrong end of the stick!

Brachiosaurus ('Arm Lizard') – Growing to be about eighty-five foot long and with a thirty-foot neck, this giraffe-like dinosaur was a gentle herbivore, despite being one of the biggest land animals that has ever lived on Earth. Living about 150 million years ago, once it was fully grown there was nothing around that could eat it, so it lived a very long life – probably around 100 years long in fact! For a while, scientists thought that it was so big that it had to live in water or else it would be too heavy to actually move. However, the opposite has been proven to be true – if it had lived in water, the high pressure would have eventually suffocated it.

Diplodocus ('Double Beam') – If the Brachiosaurus thought of itself as long, then the Diplodocus really had something to brag about. Also at large around 150 million years ago, at full length it could be up to ninety feet long, although some scientists estimate that it could even be 170 feet long. Just think about that – it's almost twice the length of a football pitch! Although that's unlikely, it is true that the Diplodocus's extremely long neck was almost too heavy for it and it probably spent much of the time resting its neck near the ground. Most human representations have this dinosaur down as a relatively harmless giant, but evidence suggests that it could pack quite a punch if it wanted to. Its very long tail was covered in spikes and could be whipped through the air at such force that it would have sliced through anything unlucky enough to be in the way.

Oi! Get off our pitch!

Compsognathus ('Pretty Jaw') – A tiny carnivorous dinosaur that lived around 140 million years ago, at one point the Compsognathus was thought to be the smallest dinosaur to have ever lived. It wasn't, though – that honour goes to the tiny bird-like Microraptor. But the Compsothagnus was a tricky little creature that preyed on small lizards and mammals trying to hide where the bigger dinos couldn't spot them. Importantly, it's very possible, and indeed likely, that there were many, many more dinosaurs as small as these all over the place. The problem for we scientists around now is that we can only see the fossils that have survived, and it's far more likely for a massive fossil of a Diplodocus to survive millions of years *and* be found than the tiny fossil of a Compsognathus.

Tyrannosaurus rex ('Tyrant Lizard') – I have left the best for last, although I do object to being called a tyrant! We lived between sixty-eight and sixty-five million years ago until we all became extinct... well all, that is, except for lonely old me! At least I have my learnatorium and all of my Assistant Learnatours to keep me company. Growing to up to thirteen metres long, we may not have been the biggest carnivores around, but we were definitely the most fearsome. Even our puny arms were actually very strong – they were just very short. But we could hold onto prey to stop it escaping with ease. Although there was some behaviour I'm not proud of, like T-rex fighting and eating each other, you have to remember it was a different time back then. It was a 'dino eat dino' world, and only the strong survived. Now of course I am far more cultured, but no other T-rex had access to my wonderful learnatorium, so they can't really be blamed for their barbaric actions. Plus, we all have to eat, don't we?

There is just one thing that not many people know about me... I actually have feathers! But I didn't want to confuse humans, so I allow the feathers to be airbrushed out when I am being drawn.

Awesome Aquatic Animals

Most of this book has examined life on land. This is partly because both you and I are land animals, and by nature we are usually more interested in land animals than anything else. It's also partly because very few dinosaurs were marine animals and I myself am biased towards talking about my own family. However, the ocean was where life began, and still today so much of the ocean is unknown and mysterious that even I, the great Dr Dino, am constantly surprised by the new and wonderful creatures the seas throw up. But some of the best creatures to be found aren't new at all. In fact they are extremely old...

Human beings are petrified of sharks. To be fair, sharks do have enormous teeth, strong jaws, powerful bodies, and can stealthily slip through the water at great speeds. But on average only a couple of humans are killed by them each year (far fewer than by lightning strikes, bee stings or even firework accidents) while at least 100

million sharks are killed by humans each year. I think that if I were a shark I should be way more frightened of humans!

Nevertheless, if the Megalodon was around now, then even I might be a bit worried about it. Sharks were one of the first predators to develop, and while they have evolved a bit over the years, the sharks that you see around you now are pretty similar to the sharks that the dinosaurs would have lived with. Except for the Megalodon.

It could grow up to sixty feet long (and maybe even bigger), which is three times bigger than the Great White Shark today – so massive that it swallowed whales whole. It had the most powerful bite of any creature *ever* (even more than me!), and teeth almost a foot long. Fortunately, this beast, which was the biggest predator to ever live in the ocean, became extinct around 2.5 million years ago, although the Great White Shark is closely related to it, a bit like a baby brother.

Plesiosaurs ('Almost Lizards') lived at the same time as dinosaurs, first appearing a little over 200 million years ago and dying off in the great extinction event that also killed off my family. A group of marine reptiles, they had wide, flat bodies, short tails, four flippers, long necks and they were dangerous predators. While the Plesiosaurus itself, the first of its kind to be found by humans, was only around four metres long, some plesiosaurs could grow up to twenty metres long and would have been one of the most dangerous animals to have ever lived.

The strange thing about plesiosaurs is that not everybody thinks they are extinct! There are some crazy humans that truly believe they have seen some in the ocean in the last few years, and beasts like the Loch Ness Monster are supposedly ancient plesiosaurs that have survived to this day. I've run the data on the chances of this being correct through my learnatorium and the answer is in. The chances of it being true are zero per cent.

The Liopleurodon ('Smooth-Sided Teeth') was a type of plesiosaur that are called pliosaurs (much like a dinosaur is a type of archosaur). This aquatic reptile lived about 155 million years ago, and its teeth were actually very sharp, so its name doesn't make much sense. Growing to around seven metres long, this beast would have been one of the top predators of its day and had a bite so powerful that if it was alive nowadays it could bite right through a car!

If you have seen the latest *Jurassic World* (and if you have, you will know by now that I find it VERY scientifically flawed) then you will have seen the Mosasaurus leaping

out of the water to swallow a shark whole. Unfortunately, once again Hollywood lets us down – rather than growing to sixty feet as claimed in the movie, a Mosasaurus would most likely only get to forty-five feet, and it would have been far too heavy to jump out of the water like a performing dolphin.

Nevertheless, the Mosasaurus and all of its fellow mosasaurs (of which there were many, and even one, Tylosaurus, which may have been bigger than the Mosasaurus) were very successful and actually overtook the plesiosaurs as the dominant species of the sea from about ninety million years ago. Sadly, this dangerous marine reptile also succumbed to extinction along with everyone else sixty-five million years ago.

Although only about fifteen feet long and about 1,000 kilograms, the Dakosaurus ('Tearing Lizard') was a dangerous beast. It lived around 145 million years ago and was a carnivore that spent most of its time at sea, but may have crawled up onto land occasionally to look for food and to meet other Dakosauruses. With a head like a crocodile's but about twice the size, serrated teeth and a predisposition for chewing on anything it came across, this monster would have been one good reason not to go for a dip in the ocean.

Ichthyosaurs ('Fish Lizards') are very old, developing about 250 million years ago and becoming extinct about 150 million years later. Similar to dolphins and whales now (although still with very sharp teeth and aggressive attitudes), they were normally a bit smaller than their fellow marine reptiles, but there were some *very* large exceptions, like the Shastasaurus, which grew to a ridiculous twenty-one metres in length, making it the largest marine reptile ever. I feel quite small in comparison, and that's not a feeling I like!

Even with my fellow dinosaurs roaming the Earth's surface all those millions of years ago, when you think about all of the gigantic marine reptiles that were around then, I think land was the safest place to be!

Post-Dinosaur Pandemonium Part Three

This is the last chapter of all of my favourite extinct animals living in the sixty-five million years between now and the horrifying death of the dinosaurs. All of the information about these (and indeed any other animal or plant discussed in this book) comes from the painstaking study of fossils. When they spot a fossil embedded in an old rock, scientists spend days, weeks, months and even years carefully chipping and dusting away at it until the fossil is free from the rock. This is a tricky process, especially for someone like me. Claws are great for tearing into meat but it does make it difficult to really get to grips with delicate tasks like that!

The real skill comes later, though, when they have to identify the animal. By sometimes using tiny pieces of skeleton, like just a fragment of the skull for example, scientists like me are able to figure out exactly what the animal looked like, how big it was, what species it belonged to... all sorts of things. What's more, it's an evolving science, so who knows what else we might learn from the fossils we have already. After all, there's a whole world of animals out there for millions of years, and we've most likely only discovered just the tip of the iceberg.

Argentavis – This was quite some bird. In fact, it was possibly the largest bird that has ever flown, with a wingspan of up to twenty-six feet, which is twice as big as any bird alive today and as big as some planes! It lived in South America about six million years ago and was a terrifying predator (like any good dinosaur should be), gliding over the heads of its prey before swooping down with its enormous talons and beak. And because it was so big, nothing could hunt it, which meant that it could live to up to around 100 years old.

Brontotherium – Known as the Thunder Beast, this enormous animal lived around thirty-five million years ago and it looked a little bit like a modern day rhino. It could grow to be five metres long, but it only ate plants and, even though it had a massive horn on the top of its head, it probably wasn't too aggressive. It also had an extremely small brain, so it probably wasn't the brightest animal in the herd either!

Andrewsarchus – Despite its boring name (it was discovered by a fellow called Andrew), this is one of my favourite of all of the animals of this period, if not my favourite overall. It lived between forty-five and thirty-five million years ago and it was probably the largest carnivorous land mammal to have ever lived, at thirteen foot long and up to 1,000 kilograms in weight. Still tiny compared to me, of course, but impressive nonetheless. Although they looked and acted like wolves and hyenas, they had hooves rather than claws, and are actually most closely related to sheep! All the same, these beasts should certainly not be under-estimated, because they were fast, powerful, and their jaws were strong enough to bite through pretty much anything. To give you an example of how tough they were, they probably hunted slow-witted brontotherium, which, despite being a bit thick, were still pretty big and hard!

Gigantopithecus – Bigfoot and the Yeti never existed, but the gigantopithecus wasn't far off. This 540 kilogram, three-metre-tall ape was probably the largest primate ever to have lived, dwarfing even the largest gorillas around today. This massive monkey lived for millions of years but became extinct about 300,000 years ago, probably when its food supply, tough plants like bamboo, disappeared from the Asian mountains where it lived.

Agriotherium – Dying off about two million years ago, this was one of the largest bears that ever lived, although it looked a bit like a cross between a modern-day dog and a bear. Growing to eight feet in size and weighing about 500 kilograms, it would have been a pretty frightening animal to come across. However, the chances are that this beast was actually a fairly slow and non-aggressive type. But you had to beware if you did get caught – scientists believe that it had the strongest bite of any land mammal to have ever lived. If it did catch you then it could probably bite right through you, bones and all, with one gnash of its teeth.

Titanis – The titanis was one of a group of birds nicknamed the 'terror birds'. All you need to know about them is in the name really… they were absolutely terrifying! (Not to me, of course. I'm a tough and brave T-rex. You humans on the other hand always go running as soon as anything exciting comes near you, such as a bear or a lion.) The titanis lived about five million years ago, and only became extinct as late as 15,000 years before now, during which time it was one of the most fearsome predators of South America. Built a bit like an ostrich, but more muscular, three metres tall and with a huge, wickedly curved beak, this bird could run at speeds of up to sixty-five kilometres per hour, easily chasing down anything that was unlucky enough to be spotted by it.

Kairuku – Another giant penguin which lived in New Zealand about twenty-seven million years ago, the kairuku was about the same size as the anthropornis that we came across earlier, being about two metres tall. The best thing about it, though, was that it had an awesomely sharp beak, which it would literally spear fish with, before gulping them down.

Smilodon – Better known as the sabre-toothed tiger, the smilodon wasn't actually a tiger. It was only distantly related to modern-day tigers, so scientifically it should just be called a cat. This stocky predator only became extinct about 10,000 years ago, and humans definitely crossed path with these beasts many times. The most distinctive feature of the smilodon was of course its teeth – the two massive teeth it used to chomp on its prey were over a foot long and dangerously sharp. Bizarrely, though, the animal's jaws were actually quite weak, so it couldn't bite very hard at all. It simply used its teeth as spears and, alongside its strong claws, this was more than enough to deal with pretty much anything that crossed its path.

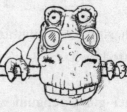

Crippling Cats

The smilodon was the most famous of the dangerous cats around in prehistoric times, but it was by no means the only one. There have been dozens of different dangerous cats around over the last few million years, but two other notable examples are the megantereon and the homotherium, who lived between ten million and 10,000 years ago. These beasts had long teeth, too, and they would pounce on their prey, often from trees, puncturing them with their teeth and then backing off while they waited for the wounded animal to bleed to death.

Humans eventually hunted all of these big cats until they were extinct, but they definitely had a battle on their hands. There has been at least one skull of a hominid (an early human) found with puncture wounds in it from the dangerous megantereon.

Gigantophis – This is one reptile that even I wouldn't have liked to have come across. It was a ten-metre-long snake that lived about forty million years ago and squeezed the life out of everything it came across, including some of the truly enormous beasts we have already come across. It is far bigger than any snake alive now, and it was thought to be the biggest snake of all time until...

Titanoboa – Coming in at a massive thirteen metres, the recently discovered titanoboa, which lived sixty million years ago, was truly colossal. So big, in fact, that it had to live underwater. This was partly because no prey lived on land at that `point that was big enough to feed it (this was right after all of the dinosaurs had tragically been wiped out), but also because it was so heavy that if it lived on land then its body would have actually crushed its internal organs! That's big.

Woolly Mammoth – Possibly the most famous of all the prehistoric animals, these shaggy elephant-like mammals only became extinct about 3,700 years ago after being hunted to death by humans (yet another magnificent species that humans have destroyed!). Despite being about four metres tall and having tusks five metres long(!) these were fairly gentle animals that lived off grass and other vegetation. We know an awful lot about these marvellous creatures because when a number of them died they ended up freezing in the northern permafrosts of Siberia. When they were found, they hadn't decomposed at all, but looked pretty much exactly as they did when they died all those millennia ago. Apart from just being quite cool (well, freezing actually) this also meant that the DNA of those frozen animals had survived... which means it is theoretically possible that we scientists could resurrect the mammoth from the dead. Whether that's a good idea or not is another question entirely.

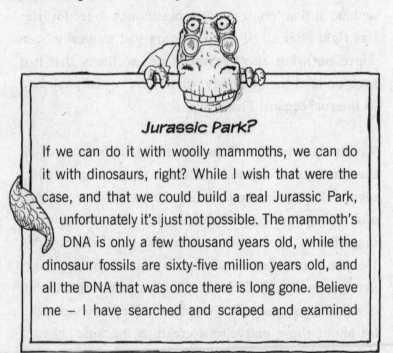

Jurassic Park?

If we can do it with woolly mammoths, we can do it with dinosaurs, right? While I wish that were the case, and that we could build a real Jurassic Park, unfortunately it's just not possible. The mammoth's DNA is only a few thousand years old, while the dinosaur fossils are sixty-five million years old, and all the DNA that was once there is long gone. Believe me – I have searched and scraped and examined those fossils myself millions of times. Unless science evolves dramatically in a way that nobody can predict, the only dinosaurs on Earth are just going to be the birds and the great Dr Dino in my learnatorium.

Quiz

1. What fictional creature is the Gigantopithecus like?
   A. The Loch Ness Monster; B. Dracula; C. Bigfoot;
   D. The Sphinx.

2. How old is the Earth?
   A. 3 million years; B. 4.5 billion years; C. 15,000
   years; D. 16 trillion years.

3. What does Tyrannosaurus rex mean?
   A. King of the Lizards; B. Short-armed Lizard;
   C. Brainy Lizard; D. Tyrant Lizard.

4. The Psittacosaurus, known as the parrot lizard, was a
   dinosaur with a body covered in what?
   A. Warts; B. Razor-sharp serrated spikes; C. Multi-
   coloured fur; D. Hedgehog-like bristles.

5. What did humans use the Glyptodon's body for before it went extinct 10,000 years ago?
   A. Its shell as shelter; B. Its tusks as spears; C. Its hooves as shoes; D. Its skin as clothes.

6. What is the tuatara famous for?
   A. Being the biggest lizard ever on land; B. Having the sharpest teeth ever; C. Being unchanged since it lived with the dinosaurs 200 million years ago; D. It used to steal T-rex eggs to munch on.

7. What did the Parasaurolophus use its hollow crest on the top of its head for?
   A. To communicate with; B. As a snorkel; C. To tickle bigger dinosaurs with; D. To breathe through.

8. How was the Moon formed?
   A. By aliens; B. It was a massive asteroid that stopped and was caught by the Earth's gravity; C. Dinosaur scientists created it; D. It was a chunk blown off the earth when another planet collided with it.

9. How big was a Stegosaurus's brain?
   A. Twice the size of a walnut; B. The size of a large pineapple; C. The size of a pea; D. The size of a football.

10. What made the Shastasaurus special?

A. It was the largest marine reptile ever; B. It was a giant crocodile as big as a whale; C. It's still around today in the deep ocean; D. It was so clever it built basic underwater huts.

11. Why would a Phosphatherium be frightened by modern elephants?

A. Elephants hunted them until they went extinct; B. They were scared of the colour grey; C. They were mini-elephants, only two feet big; D. All of the above.

12. What was Toba?

A. The name of the last T-rex – my mother; B. A supervolcano that erupted 70,000 years ago and almost killed off humans; C. A species of mammals that humans descended from; D. The dinosaur version of the tuba.

13. What did *Jurassic Park* get wrong about Velociraptors?

A. They had feathers; B. They were much smaller; C. They weren't all that intelligent (especially compared to me); D. All of the above.

14. What were archosaurs?
   A. Dinosaurs arch-nemesis; B. What dinosaurs evolved into; C. The scientific term for dinosaurs and other animals related to them; D. Flying dinosaurs.

15. How old is the oldest living thing that humans have ever found?
   A. 300 million years; B. 3.5 billion years; C. 1.2 trillion years; D. 40,000 years.

16. What sort of mammal did all other mammals evolve from sixty-five million years ago?
   A. A rat-like shrew; B. A tiger-like cat; C. An aggressive miniature bear; D. A camel-like pony.

17. In what way did human scientists try to slander the dinosaur Oviraptor?
   A. They said it ate humans; B. They said it ate its own children; C. They said it was the weakest dinosaur that ever lived; D. They said it stole the eggs of other dinosaurs.

18. The Presbyornis was a giant mixture of which modern-day creatures?
   A. A hippo, a rhino and a giraffe; B. A goose, a duck

and a flamingo; C. A cat, a dog and a hamster; D. A pony, a cow and a kangaroo.

19. What was horrible about the mammal cimexomys?
A. It was voted the ugliest animal to have ever lived; B. Its poo was so pungent it could be smelled a mile away; C. It used to eat dinosaur's eggs; D. It used to tease innocent dinosaur children.

20. What confused humans scientists about the 20-inch tall Archaeopteryx?
A. They didn't think dinosaurs could be so small; B. They incorrectly thought it was the very first bird; C. A fossil of it was found with a bullet hole, indicating it had only just been killed; D. Humans are simply easily confused because of their limited brain power compared to myself.

Answers

1.	C	9.	A	17.	D
2.	B	10.	A	18.	B
3.	D	11.	C	19.	C
4.	D	12.	B	20.	B
5.	A	13.	D		(although
6.	C	14.	C		D is fairly
7.	A	15.	B		accurate as
8.	D	16.	A		well)

Also available in this series:

How Fast Can You Fart?

The wildest, weirdest, funniest,
grossest, fastest, longest, brainiest and
best facts about history, science, food
geography, words, and much more!
ISBN: 978 1 78219 766 9
£5.99

Did Romans Really Wash Themselves in Wee?

The wackiest, wittiest, filthiest,
foulest, oldest, wisest and best facts
about history!
ISBN: 978 1 78219 915 1
£5.99